I0437411

"WISE SAYINGS"
My Mother Taught Me

"WISE SAYINGS"
My Mother Taught Me

Linda Nichols Gomes

Copyright © 2009 by Linda Nichols Gomes.

ISBN: Hardcover   978-1-4363-6684-7
            Softcover   978-1-4363-6683-0

All rights reserved. No part of this book may be reproduced or transmitted in any form or by any means, electronic or mechanical, including photocopying, recording, or by any information storage and retrieval system, without permission in writing from the copyright owner.

This book was printed in the United States of America.

To order additional copies of this book, contact:
Xlibris Corporation
1-888-795-4274
www.Xlibris.com
Orders@Xlibris.com
45569

For
Joseph and Stella Nichols
Lonny Gomes
Lonny, Jr
Joshua
and
Benjamin

ACKNOWLEDGMENTS

This book is dedicated to my parents,
Stella Best Nichols and Joseph Nathaniel Nichols, Sr.—

I honor you by giving back much of what you have instilled
in me during your nearly fifty-nine years of marriage.
I love you dearly.

To my husband, Lonny, for being my biggest supporter
and best friend—
Thanks for encouraging me in this endeavor;
I love you, Pooh!
And to our three sons, Lonny, Jr., Joshua and Benjamin—
It has been a joy raising you and a blessing to see
the fine men you have become. You are our greatest
accomplishment!

A special thanks to my sisters,
Esther A. Splaine and Mayetta L. Brown for their belief
in this manuscript and for their insightful and inspiring
guidance in the editing of this book.
I am grateful to you for your love and support.

PREFACE

This book was written in honor of my mother, Stella Best Nichols, who died on January 2, 2006 at the age of 82. Stella and Joseph Nichols raised eleven children in the city of Cambridge, Massachusetts. All eleven children were involved in the Arts, played musical instruments, graduated from college, and are professionals who contribute positively to our society.

If you would have been able to speak with my mother, she would have told you that she enjoyed every moment of raising her children . . . and especially loved the summers when she could instill more wisdom, knowledge, stories and time in them. (I personally have fond memories of her teaching us to square dance on the back porch!)

My mother had a strong faith in God, and she relied on that faith to give her wisdom in raising her children. Every morning, prior to school, she would sit us down before breakfast, and give us a "Wise Saying" to memorize and "live out" for the week. These are some of those bits of wisdom.

♥ I wrote a poem in 2004 in honor of my parents, and included it at the end of this book.

My mother loved this poem, and requested that it be read at her funeral.

HOW TO USE THIS BOOK

This is a Character Education book, and can be used by parents or teachers to implant "wisdom" in their children. I have utilized these "Wise Sayings" at home and in my classroom, and have seen wonderful positive changes in my children and students' behavior; they have begun to take ownership of their actions and they freely share their experiences with their classmates.

In order to use this book effectively:

- The teacher or parent should choose *one "Wise Saying"* per week; choose those that fit your class climate or situation. (For unity across the curriculum, it is best if all classes work on the same "Wise Saying" each week—there are eighty from which to choose.)
- The teacher reads, and then has the class repeat the "Wise Saying" a couple of times in unison.
- The teacher asks a few students (by the raising of a hand) to explain or to give an example of what the "Wise Saying" means to them (this gives them ownership)
- If you, as the teacher or parent, have an example, you may briefly share your experience with the children (students feel more connected to you as a fellow human being!)

- Encourage students to "live out" these sayings during the week by *doing* what they say!
- Always leave room for the children to share their experiences.
- Reward students with verbal praise when you see them "living out" a "Wise Saying".

♥ This should take from five to six minutes at the beginning of the day or at the beginning of each class and then move on to your daily curriculum. As they learn to "live out" more "Wise Sayings" each week, students will enthusiastically share their experiences!

Many times, all I need to say to a misbehaving student is: "Are you acting wisely?" and I see an immediate change in the behavior.

Here are several examples of student responses in my classroom:

"I'm sorry, Mrs. G, I wasn't acting wisely."

"I'm learning to control my temper!"

"I blew it 'cause I got mad when my Mom corrected me, but then I told her I was sorry."

"This girl who was mean to me fell and hurt herself, and I helped her up because I remembered that we shouldn't take pleasure in someone's misfortune!"

I was at a store and started to steal something, but then I remembered that wise people think before they act, and I put it back!"

I don't yell at my Mom any more because wise people think before they speak, and I really want to be a wise person!"

A parent recently told me: "You're doing a great job, keep it up! My daughter's attitude is really changing!"

♥ I hope that you and your students enjoy using this book as much as I enjoyed writing it!

A
GENTLE
ANSWER
CALMS
ANGER

A GOSSIP CAN NEVER KEEP A SECRET

A HARSH ANSWER STIRS UP ANGER

ALWAYS DO WHAT IS RIGHT AND FAIR

ALWAYS REMEMBER THE THINGS YOU HAVE BEEN TAUGHT

ANGER IS CRUEL AND DESTRUCTIVE

AN IMPATIENT
PERSON GETS
INTO TROUBLE

A PERSON, NOT THINKING, WILL WALK RIGHT INTO TROUBLE AND REGRET IT LATER

A TRUE FRIEND GIVES AN HONEST ANSWER

AVOID

PEOPLE

WHO HAVE

HOT

TEMPERS

A WISE PERSON WANTS TO LEARN

BE CAREFUL HOW YOU THINK – YOUR LIFE IS SHAPED BY YOUR THOUGHTS

BE CAREFUL WHAT YOU SAY

BEING

CHEERFUL

KEEPS YOU

HEALTHY

BE SMART, AND OBEY THE LAW

CHOOSE YOUR FRIENDS WISELY

DON'T BE JEALOUS OF FOOLISH PEOPLE

DON'T
"GET EVEN"
WITH
SOMEONE—
FORGIVE THEM

DON'T TAKE PLEASURE IN SOMEONE'S MISFORTUNE

DON'T TRY TO ACT LIKE FOOLISH PEOPLE

DO
YOURSELF A
FAVOR
AND
LEARN ALL
YOU CAN

FOLLOW THE EXAMPLE OF WISE PEOPLE

FOOLISH

PEOPLE ARE

SATISFIED

WITH

IGNORANCE

GETTING
WISDOM
IS THE MOST
IMPORTANT
THING
YOU CAN DO

GET WISDOM, AND
YOU HAVE A
BRIGHT FUTURE

GIVE
SERIOUS
THOUGHT
TO
THE WAY
YOU
LIVE

HAVING WISDOM CAN MAKE YOUR LIFE PLEASANT

HOT TEMPERS CAUSE ARGUMENTS

IF ALL YOU DO IS EAT AND SLEEP, YOU WILL SOON BE WEARING RAGS

IF YOU ARE SENSIBLE, YOU WILL CONTROL YOUR TEMPER

IF YOU ARE WISE, YOU WILL PAY ATTENTION WHEN YOU ARE CORRECTED

IF YOU ARE
WRONG,
ADMIT IT

IF YOU **BRAG** ALL THE TIME, YOU ARE ASKING FOR TROUBLE

IF YOU LISTEN TO
WISDOM, YOU
WILL KNOW
WHAT IS RIGHT

IF YOU LISTEN TO WISDOM, YOU WILL KNOW WHAT YOU SHOULD DO

IT IS BETTER TO BE A PATIENT PERSON THAN A POWERFUL PERSON

LEARN TO CONTROL YOUR ANGER

LISTEN

BEFORE

YOU

GIVE AN

ANSWER

LIVE WISELY, SO YOUR PARENTS CAN BE PROUD OF YOU

NEVER
BOAST
ABOUT
TOMORROW

NEVER FORGET THE WISDOM YOU HAVE LEARNED

NEVER LET GO

OF LOYALTY

AND

FAITHFULNESS

NEVER
SAY
THINGS
THAT
AREN'T
TRUE

NOTHING
YOU
COULD
WANT
CAN
COMPARE
WITH
WISDOM

PAY CLOSE ATTENTION WHEN YOU ARE CORRECTED

PEOPLE WITH HOT TEMPERS DO FOOLISH THINGS

PEOPLE WHO
SET
TRAPS FOR
OTHERS
GET CAUGHT
THEMSELVES

PEOPLE WHO WASTE TIME WILL ALWAYS BE POOR

PLAN AHEAD AND GET GOOD ADVICE

SENSIBLE PEOPLE ARE PATIENT

SENSIBLE PEOPLE WILL SEE TROUBLE COMING AND AVOID IT

SOMETIMES, IT TAKES A PAINFUL EXPERIENCE TO MAKE US CHANGE OUR WAYS

SPEAK KIND WORDS TO OTHERS

STAY AWAY FROM **BAD** PEOPLE—THEY HAVE NOTHING **GOOD** TO TEACH YOU

STAY
AWAY
FROM
GOSSIP

THOSE
WHO
BECOME
WISE
ARE
HAPPY

TREAT OTHERS THE WAY YOU WANT TO BE TREATED

TRUSTWORTHY PEOPLE DO NOT TELL LIES

WHEN BAD
PEOPLE
TEMPT YOU,
**DON'T
GIVE IN**

WHEN YOU ARE CORRECTED, TAKE IT AS A WARNING

WISDOM CAN LEAD YOU SAFELY THROUGH LIFE

WISDOM IS MORE VALUABLE THAN JEWELS

WISDOM, TRUTH, LEARNING AND GOOD SENSE ARE VALUABLE THINGS

WISE
PEOPLE
ACCEPT
GOOD
ADVICE

WISE
PEOPLE
ARE
CAREFUL
TO
STAY OUT
OF
TROUBLE

WISE
PEOPLE
CONTROL
THEIR
ANGER

WISE

PEOPLE

CONTROL

THEIR

TEMPER

WISE
PEOPLE
DO
WHAT IS
RIGHT

WISE
PEOPLE
PAY
ATTENTION
AND LEARN
ALL THEY
CAN

WISE
PEOPLE
SEE TROUBLE
COMING
AND
AVOID IT

WISE PEOPLE STAY OUT OF ARGUMENTS

WISE PEOPLE THINK BEFORE THEY ACT

WISE
PEOPLE
THINK
BEFORE
THEY
ANSWER

WISE

PEOPLE

THINK

BEFORE

THEY

SPEAK

WISE PEOPLE TELL THE TRUTH

WISE
PEOPLE
WATCH
THEIR
STEP

WISE PEOPLE WILL LEARN FROM WHAT THEY ARE TAUGHT

YOU ARE HURTING YOURSELF IF YOU REFUSE TO LEARN

YOU CANNOT HIDE FROM YOUR CONSCIENCE

YOUR
EDUCATION
IS YOUR LIFE

—

<u>GUARD IT</u>
<u>WELL</u>

STELLA AND JOE ©2006

By Linda Nichols Gomes

Not "Once upon a time" or "A long time ago",
But I'm telling the *true* story of Stella and Joe.

They started life together in the year of forty-seven
With only four hundred 'bucks' and lots of faith in God
in Heaven.

Stella was a housewife, and Joe was a tailor,
He had just finished service as a U.S. sailor.

They started life simple, with a little tailor shop;
With their expertise and hard work, things began to "hop"!

Now, every day, back and forth—this was their pace,
Until one day in March, Stella slowed down in the "race".

Their first child was born—Esther Alberta was her name . . .
She was 'cute as a button" and such a feisty little dame!

Some time later, here came another,
Esther called Joseph Junior by the name of "Brother".

Then John Henry was born, and Mayetta Louise—
Joining this growing family, and making it a tight squeeze!

They bought a big old farmhouse in the North
end of the town
Of Cambridge, Massachusetts, putting
hard-earned money down.

Every day they worked long hours at home
}and in their shop.
Late at night Joe came home weary;
he'd eat and want to drop!

But they'd work some more in spite of being
'Oh, so very tired',
That big old farmhouse they just bought
still had to be rewired!

Joe and Stella had talked of having four
and then no more—
But it seems that God in Heaven had
much more for them in store!

Paul was born, then Robert, and along came Richard Kevin—
They both said "Eight will be enough;
it's time that we were quittin'!"

Linda Ann, the eighth, was born in the middle of a gale,
The weatherman said, "Don't come out
tonight in all this hail!"

But go out they did, in the midst of all,
and it was worth the fight—
For all their labor, that girl-child was born
in the middle of the night!

After the eighth, they lost a child, '
twas a sad road they trod;
Stella and Joe committed that soul
to the loving hands of God.

After a year had passed and gone, Gail Edith,
the ninth, was born;
Then two years later, a little boy
named Glen Allen came along.

Karen Arlene was the very last, born this side of Heaven.
"I'm done", said Stella, "There will be no more;
we're stopping at eleven!"

Another turn in the road was ahead
when Karen became deaf,
Her unexpected handicap left us all bereft.

But all the family worked together
to help with this special need;
With perseverance on everyone's part,
at age four, Karen began to read.

Now with their family all in tow,
they gave them all they could,
Music, sports, church, school,
and chores kept them busy doing "good".

But most of all, this family had God
as their "Unseen Guest",
"If you put the Lord first",
said Stella and Joe, "He will take care of the rest".

Down through the years there were ups and downs and
many joys and sorrows,
Like any other family there were hopes
of bright tomorrows.

The children grew up, and one by one,
off to college they went,
Most of them got scholarships,
so not too much money was spent.

Esther became a Registered Nurse
and Joe a Speech Therapist,
John, the "Artist Extraordinaire"
was a Clinical Psychologist.

Mayetta, nicknamed "Cissie", is a Special Education Teacher,
And Paul, who went to Harvard,
is a Professor and published Author.

Robert is a Master Electrician,
Richard Kevin a Phys Ed Teacher,
Linda teaches Music and is a Women's Retreat speaker.

Gail, like her older sister, teaches Special Ed,
Glen, a financial broker, is really 'knockin' 'em dead"!

Karen went to Gallaudet and majored in Social Work,
As a student and a Mom of three, she has no time to shirk.

The children have moved and live in Maryland,
Rhode Island and Indiana;
As far west as Hawaii and Colorado,
in Massachusetts, and South Carolina.

Everyone is married with children
or with 'grandkids' in tow . . .
Who would have thought this would all come about
From the lives of Stella and Joe!

www.ingramcontent.com/pod-product-compliance
Lightning Source LLC
Chambersburg PA
CBHW031254280526
45784CB00004B/1851